**This book was made possible to print the way life aligns with lessons.**

**Thank you to those who have helped:**

Chris McCandless

Mike

Mom, Dad

My siblings

Paula Piscopo

Nick Colevas

Yvonne Stephens

Randy Minish

book formatting done by:

*Stay diligent,*
*stay patient,*
*stay elated.*

*Stay writing.*

*Stay mindful and aware of its tricks, and also its growth and its function inside of you.*
*Of this process as a whole——as practice, a bound unit that cannot be divided,*
*but told as Truth, as shape, and as form*
*——because you remember why you love it,*
*as though that is its only rule.*

*This, too, will tell time.*

# waiting on rocks for boats

A Poetic Memoir,
by Paige VanSice

*1.*

*(Because of Birth)*

They scrubbed the yellow from the walls when Grandma passed,
when smoking took her lungs, when I remember seeing dad cry.
There is memory of her elbows: the work bone—old and purple, skin thin as wet paper,
her smile and its spaces, like piano teeth.
Dad has exactly her mouth's shape and I remember when they're happy how their faces lift.
I told other people she died in my arms,
because I did not know her like other kids knew Grandmas.

 

 

I knew mom's dad had died when we got his couch
Because three packs a day,
the Hamburger,
Velveeta.
Because he drank the Listerine
when they hid the booze.
He loved in unconditional ways.

His couch came to Antrim Street,
in the 90s when we rag-rolled walls.
Chihuahua, Dachshund, Pekingese, off the tongue like "mutt".
The house they would gut when the termites were found.
The house I would look from in autumns and in winters,
a birthday in spring,
because we left for summers.

I'm ten years old in a purple track suit on a stone-laid porch that dad built.
The steps are cracked after years of ollies and bike tires,
and my little brother and I play Jacks on the chipped ledges
while our parents pack the van with the mattress,
 because we left for summers.

Because home is home to Sitka spruce

Home, where Fast Car goes.

4,000 miles 'North To The Future':


Park's Highway,

Totem hashbrowns,

A trail called Stampede,

the Farfegnugen, the Fuji Film, the fuchsia fireweed


May to September,

rafts over rapids,

waiting on rocks for boats.

Some people are lake people,
I was a river girl.
Held tight the Nenana,
the overhead alpenglow,
the Christopher Cross, the Steeley Dan,
the alligator comb.

        The Eagles', Desperado, says, "you're a hard one",
        battery to wire from a tape deck dad installed.
        It is loud over 'L' and 'M' and the number '7'
        ------Sesame Street-smarts in VHS grain.

        I put three plastic pizzas onto three plastic plates,

        because when I played waitress I knew I was mom,
        and when I played mom I knew I was tough.

        The way you are tough when you bathe your kids
        in a tub without its water,
        on land without its power,
        because tough is when you choose that.

>Dad was bravery's face,
>tough like hide because it had to be
>brave.
>
>Strong,
>like coffee black,
>like when varnish hits a nose.
>
>Because he knew houses.

Because word about the body of a boy in a bus made Fairbanks news in '92.
67 pounds and one-hundred days alone,
because wild does not mean company,
because that is why he left.

Because dead as meat is to be declared,
as nuisance, as pieces
In a story that is read, as words that are written.
"Be it no concern
Point of no return"

>I trembled from the hands at the table during grace,
>back when we were saying grace,
>when that was what we did,
>
>because we went in spurts.

Because I am 15 and feeding the old in dining rooms from wheelchairs.
7AMs all smell the same; pulverized meats and sickening sweets,
because who were they to care after taste buds lose their luster.
My stomach is oatmeal and Patsy Cline in dining rooms sings,
*Three Cigarettes In An Ashtray.*


Because of soaps and how they smell,
and the process on the faces of the bodies with the hands that use the soap,
how we choose our scents so wisely and for the seasons.


                        Because of carrots and our eyes

                        A prayer everyday

                        Catching cold from the weather

                        Making faces that will stay

Mom had tomatoes that Michigan summer,
because she liked having color, she said.
On her skin and in her salads.
Said I'd never taste the full bouquet
of a tomato from the fridge,
so we keep them on the counter.


The neighborhood of the library in the town I grew
Is childhood Halloweens as a flapper, then a bride
Dirt Earth and dry leaf
Bit-o-Honey and Bazooka
Muddying make-up under moonlight


The tag said Grandpa Sonny,
the way families cover for Santa Claus.
He was belly and thumb,
chewed steak through gum,
he was the chair in the room down the hall.


Art on walls, signed
Ola, Pooch, Dave
flora, faces, fauna
oil, leather, lathe

A college roommate bakes breads and I smell them and I listen to her stories about public transportation. Her latest batch of Kombucha tea grows menacingly in a jar by the sink. It is bubbling, it is breathing. I'm convinced it hears us speak.

She offers coffee and I take it.

Black,

"like my dad," I say.

> We are nervous and unslept around the caverns of eyes,
> because we are clocked and on budgets
>
> Because time is always money,
> we will never have the time,
> never have the cash
>
> We chomp at bits
> Dried and jerked from freezers
> Time in coffee cans

Because of shape
Because of size
Because Gestalt,
whole as round as globe.
Whole as a sum, a meaningful unit.

When calls tally care,
I begin not to care
the shape or the size of the mark
that is meant to keep whole
while tallying cares

I was told to suck in my gut.

Followed, were:

        Guts.

        Heart,

        sense,

        eyeballs, to see Truth.

Left to shake, to tremble:

        It was guttural---it was,

        and it was visceral---it was,

        But not 'Because of fat'

Because I am human and I am skeleton; muscle and bone,
here fat or thin or just simply here, and it is heft just to know this.


Because when she said "big girl" she hated to say it
Because when I said "big girl" it meant that I was grown

                And I could not blame her
                Could not blame her mother
                Or hers


If "make more to spend more" and "buy large to save large",
we have purchased our dunk tank, have signed for defeat

And there are no last meals in Texas,
because of buying time

And time was still money,
And timing never right

Because control and its settings; auto-pilot and speed
Convenience as troubling in short-cuts

Memorizing moments
to the tune of
L
M
N
O
P (for Paige and for Parker)

X
Y (You are Yours)
Signed Sincerely,
                Z

Because when everyone I know is bringing casserole,
we are all guppies here.

They spoke about freedom tucked into penciled skirts,
when they had no choice when that sounded like freedom.

But dogma does not decide when we rise from what is tucked
Rise, to brighten time with battered innards

I was clay, a new babe,

and like the pressure for juice an orange knows,

led self through the dark as though it saw.

*2.*

*(Because of Truth)*

Because before I left, I was told I'd come back skinny,
the way people say it like that is all I'd need.
And I was less fat when I returned,
but no one knew what I'd need.


I had forgotten what it was like to feel free.
Because stagnancy is dust that does not lift itself.
Because of its weight,
the way it fits into jeans.


Because McCandless had done it because Tolstoy had done it.
Because "fear is at the root of bad writing", and so I could not fear.

Because comfort came to me unmanaged, like a tangled mane snapping and breaking at its roots. I wandered into Truth as I did the tundra—-disconnected from pavements, and so, from fiction. I clung to renewal, of actualizing something less external, seeded deep, in the darkest pits of self,

of turning a psychical corner,

of becoming hard to recognize.

The empiricist in these bones says that Truth is found in trees and in winds and on the paper in journals that solidify fear because they are my own. I was not told to figure things out, or that help was on its way.


And then is when I found it.

The complication with perception is that

we are complicated and we perceive.

the heat from our fire,

the start of the chain.


I tone bit by bit to match my insides
Good as new,
survival of a maniac.


And I ask myself,


is it thick,
that our skin is supposed to be
when we are tough?

Because I cannot remember if I am acting tough or that I am actually tough.
Because it is meant to penetrate thick skin.

The years that have aged me,
I see it in eyes,
in ways I see Truth,

in ways I see October;
trees like raging oceans,
losing leaves to the sea.

They warned me of the rain out west

-----said it'd make me depressed

In the north, while they shoveled it frozen.




                            Winter,

                Your heaving coats, your ice moats
                We love in different ways

Divorce made me cry at Bob Dylan's, *Girl of the North Country,*
and go to the gym most mornings.

There were no longer phone plans,
or love in our eyes.

And so it goes.


He was soft of dough,
of soups that stay a simmer
He was gentle like pastry encased
Not ready to rescue
burning loaves from bread ovens,
Yank a timer from its box
I was fingertips to frying pans,
nowhere to take the heat


I should have seen the warning sun blazing.

If happiness real when shared,
perhaps then,
sadness too

Like Band-Aids from old wounds


Because Jung and his balance
Because Locke and his slate

Cold positions on an outhouse seat:
When compromise means to weaken, I do not consider it weak.

We board the S.S. Rational: a ship against subjective glaciers
Where we all learn to sink or to swim,
because lifeguards need lifeguards,
like dentists need dentists.
To see things from the inside.

When jingoists are heroes, I have no heroes
because we are shame
And so they say,
"Serve God to seek Truth"
and
"We told you so"
Because I am now not my own to decide

To wear blinders, black as coal

To prime; a preparatory coat

Guilt as extrusion

Food as filler

Mosquitoes under tongues,

an invisible wretch

Like waiting on birthdays for birthdays to happen,
because then and now and always we will wait.

Little brothers as heroes
No flags to wave
Repaid in ways of big sisters

And as Earth is mother,
Fire is father

Dad got cancer and the news burned like throats
Like blue Basics and hot pop bottles
Like work trucks in the sun
Sawdust stuck to stains

And because we are VanSice,
we compare tough skin

We pull it far from our skeletons

August sun

Sation, repeat

Rising, blazing, sleeping

Fruit after heat

Like peaches that cling

Wave tide and the moon

Autumn, soon

We pressed the juice
from pome fruit
Sipping Northern Spy
Hudson's Golden Gem
long into fall
In cold,
when things become hard


Like brothers in blizzards,
we rally through time
Without sight,
likes clothes to the Emperor

Because we patch like we cannot have holes, like they do not help to filter
Gold from soil, a rock from its hard place
We edit as procedure,
Blanket to cover,
Sugar to sweeten


But cavities undetected, still the rot
No whitening can make bright

He cuts her methadone into halves and my crying eyes read *'A Dying Experience'*
while he makes her the sandwiches she cannot keep down.
I don't see her in the living room,
because that is where you live.


Because when she passed she stopped breathing
and he knew because he no longer heard it.
In the way she said goodbye.

When I said I was dead inside
Last year, November
I was not laughing,
and he knew
Today I am shrinking,
as tomorrow takes room,
because love adjusts in these ways


I saw the light today.


In a south running river
sourced from the north

In the light,

she was strong from her insides,

from Truth that billows in silence;

the aftermath of bombs.


A reminder what is gained,

living uncomfortable years.

-About the Author-

Paige VanSice is wanderer and writer. She is what she wants to be when she grows up. She is inspired by feeling the smallness in mountains and the power from rivers. Paige is an undergraduate of Eastern Michigan's Creative Writing program, and attributes finding the purpose in her passion, to telling time by finding Truth. This is her first published work.

www.ingramcontent.com/pod-product-compliance
Lightning Source LLC
Chambersburg PA
CBHW022000290426
44108CB00012B/1155